TRUE STORIES ABOUT
ABRAHAM LINCOLN

by RUTH BELOV GROSS

SCHOLASTIC INC.
New York Toronto London Auckland Sydney

For Willy,
with all my love

ISBN 0-590-43754-2

12 11 10 9 8 7 6 5 4 3 2 1   9/8 0 1 2 3/9

CONTENTS

The pictures in this book are woodcuts. They were made many years ago by Charles Turzak. Charles Turzak lived in Illinois, where Abraham Lincoln lived for part of his life.

A NEW BABY

On February 12, 1809, a boy baby was born in Kentucky. He was born in a little cabin made of logs.

"We'll name him Abraham," his parents said. But mostly they called him Abe.

Abe was the second baby in the family. His parents, Nancy and Tom Lincoln, already had a little girl. Her name was Sarah.

The cabin where the Lincolns lived was very small. It had only one room. And it was not a very big room.

The cabin had just one window, and the floor was made of dirt.

DENNIS HANKS MEETS HIS NEW COUSIN

The day the baby was born, nine-year-old Dennis Hanks ran through the woods to the Lincoln cabin. Dennis could hardly wait to see his new little cousin.

When he got there he took a long look at the baby. It was all red and wrinkled. Dennis thought the baby's skin looked like squeezed cherries.

After a while, Dennis asked if he could hold the baby.

"Be careful, Dennis," Nancy Lincoln said. "You are the first boy he's ever seen." Then she gave him the baby to hold.

Dennis took the baby in his arms. Little Abe began to cry, and he wouldn't stop.

Dennis handed the yowling baby back. "Aunt, take him!" he said. "He'll never come to much!"

The baby grew very fast. Soon he was crawling, and then he was walking. Tom Lincoln looked at his son and joked about the way little Abe's long legs were getting longer and longer.

When Abe was seven, Tom Lincoln began to talk about moving to a new state called Indiana. Land was cheap there, people said. Maybe the Lincolns could live better in Indiana.

So the Lincolns packed their pots and pans and their good feather bed and their spinning wheel. They packed their clothes and some food, and Abe's father packed his carpenter tools.

In those days, there were no trains or planes or cars. People rode horses or they rode in wagons pulled by horses. If they didn't have horses or wagons, they walked.

The Lincolns had horses. Maybe they had a wagon too, but nobody knows for sure.

They traveled for many days. They went through forests full of wild animals. In some places there wasn't even a road, and Abe's father had to chop down trees to make a path.

When the Lincolns got to Indiana, they built a new log cabin.

First they cleared away the trees and bushes and vines that covered their land. Tom Lincoln chopped down the trees, and Abe chopped away the bushes and vines.

Abe had his own axe. He was only seven, but he was big for his age. And he was very strong.

One day when Abe was almost eight, he took his father's gun and shot a wild turkey. When he saw the turkey lying dead on the ground, he felt sick. After that he never killed another animal.

Abe's mother died when he was nine years old. His sister Sarah was eleven. Together the little family buried Nancy Lincoln.

For the next year Abe and Sarah and their father were sad and lonely. Then their father went away. When he came back he brought a new wife. "Here's your new mammy," he said.

Abe and Sarah liked their stepmother right away.

Abe Lincoln went to school for a little while when he was six and when he was seven.

He went to school for a little while when he was eleven.

He went for another little while when he was thirteen.

And then he went back to school for a little while when he was fifteen.

Maybe that is why Abe Lincoln always said he went to school "by littles." All the days he went to school didn't add up to a year.

There weren't a whole lot of books around when Abe was growing up. But he read every book he could find.

Sometimes he read something that he wanted to think about. He copied it down, and then he read it over and over. When he didn't have any paper to write on, he used a board.

At night Abe did arithmetic. He sat by the fireplace and wrote numbers on the fire shovel. He added, he subtracted, he multiplied. Then he cleaned the shovel off and started all over again.

The Lincolns had their own farm in Indiana. So Abe learned to do all kinds of hard work.

He plowed fields. He planted seeds. He fed the animals. He cut the corn. He chopped down trees. And he split logs into rails.

Every farmer needed rails for making fences. Rail fences kept a farmer's horses and cows and pigs from getting loose. Rail splitting was extra-hard work, but Abe was good at it.

When Abe's father didn't need him on the farm, he sent him out to work for other people.

Some people said that Abe Lincoln was just about the best worker in Indiana. They said he could do the work of three men.

Other people said that Abe was lazy. Didn't he always have a book in his hand? And wasn't he always stopping to read, or think, or tell funny stories?

Abe had an answer for that. "My father taught me to work," he said. "But he never taught me to love it."

Abe was nineteen years old now, and he was six feet four inches tall. His stepmother liked to tease him about how tall he was.

"Abe," she used to say, "you'd better wash your head or you'll be getting dirt on my nice clean ceiling."

That gave Abe an idea. He would play a joke on his stepmother!

He got some children to squish their bare feet in a mud puddle. He picked the children up one at a time and carried them to the house.

Then he turned the children upside down and walked them across the ceiling. They left their muddy footprints right on the ceiling.

Abe's stepmother laughed when she saw what he had done.

"I ought to spank you," she said. But she wasn't really angry.

Abe laughed too. Then he got some buckets of whitewash and made the ceiling clean again.

Abe liked to read in bed at night. Every night he took a book up to bed with him and read by the light of a candle.

One night Abe was reading a book he had borrowed from a farmer. The book was a biography of George Washington. Abe read until his candle went out. Then he put the book away. He put it in a crack in the wall, between two logs.

That night it rained. The rain came right through the cracks in the wall. And by morning the farmer's book was soaking wet.

Abe didn't have any money to pay for the book. So he went to the farmer and said, "I'm a good worker. Let me work on your farm until I have paid you for the book."

Abe worked hard in the farmer's cornfield. He worked for three days. "You've done a good job," the farmer said, and he let Abe keep the book.

Abe went home with the book that night. He was happy to have another book of his own — especially a book about Washington. George Washington was one of his heroes.

MOVING TO ILLINOIS

Abe Lincoln lived in Indiana until he was twenty-one years old. Then his family moved again. This time they moved to the state of Illinois.

Abe helped his parents build a new house in Illinois. He planted corn for them. And he split hundreds of rails for the fences they needed.

Then Abe said good-bye to his father and his stepmother. He was twenty-two now. From now on he would be earning his own living.

Abe did not have any money when he left his parents. He did not even have an extra suit of clothes. All he had was a handkerchief with a few things wrapped inside.

Abe was on his own now.

At first he earned his living by doing the things he knew how to do best — chopping wood and splitting rails.

After a while, Abe got a job on a boat. He went to New Orleans with a boat full of pork and corn and live hogs. When he came back to Illinois, he got a job in a store in the town of New Salem. He sold tea and eggs and shoes and tools and hats.

The store didn't have many customers. So Abe spent a lot of time sitting under a tree near the store, reading.

One day when Abe was working in the store, a lady paid him six cents too much. That night, after the store was closed, Abe walked three miles to the lady's house. He gave her the six cents. Then he walked home again.

Soon people began to call Abe Lincoln "Honest Abe."

Denton Offutt owned the store that Abe worked in. Mr. Offutt was proud of Abe. He bragged about him all the time. "Abe Lincoln is the smartest man in the United States," Mr. Offutt would say.

Sometimes he would say, "Abe Lincoln can lift more, run faster, throw farther, jump higher, and wrestle better than any man in the county."

When a gang called the Clary's Grove Boys heard that, they said, "Prove it!" They said that their leader, Jack Armstrong, could beat Abe at wrestling any day. Abe did not want to fight—but now he had to.

On the day of the wrestling match, people came from far and near to watch. Everybody said that Jack Armstrong was as strong as an ox. Everybody said he would lick Abe Lincoln.

They wrestled for a long time, but Jack couldn't lick Abe.

At last Jack put out his hand. "Let's shake hands and call it a draw," he said. Jack Armstrong and Abe Lincoln were friends from that day on.

New Salem, where Abe Lincoln lived, was a small town. It had about twenty-five houses and a few stores. The post office was in a grocery store.

Abe became postmaster when he was twenty-four. The job didn't pay much — but it wasn't a big job, either. People came to Abe to pick up their mail or to give him the letters they wanted to send.

Abe had plenty of time to read his books and to earn extra money at other jobs. So Abe did farm work again, and he split rails. And he learned to measure land. That kind of work was called surveying.

Very often, Abe's job took him miles from the post office. If Abe happened to have a letter for somebody who lived along the way, he put the letter in his hat. When he saw the person, Abe would say, "I have some mail for you."

Then he would take off his hat and deliver the letter.

For the rest of his life, Abe Lincoln had the habit of keeping important papers in his hat.

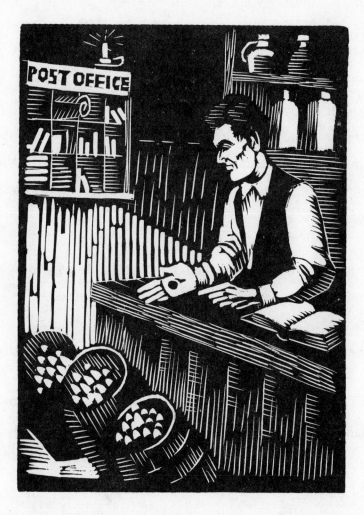

Everybody around New Salem knew the tall young man who carried letters in his hat. "Howdy, Abe," they would say. Abe Lincoln would stop and talk a while, and maybe tell a funny story.

Everybody liked Abe Lincoln. And when election time came, the people elected him to go to the state capital to help make the state's laws. So Abe became a member of the Illinois legislature when he was twenty-five.

Before the election, Abe had to tell people why they should vote for him. He made speeches, just the way people do now. But there was no radio or television then. Anybody who wanted to be elected had to go out and talk to people.

One day Abe visited a farm. He went out to the field and talked to the men who were cutting corn.

"We'll vote for you if you show us that you can cut corn," they said.

"That's easy," Abe said. He took a knife and whacked away at the corn. The men laughed, and Abe Lincoln got their votes.

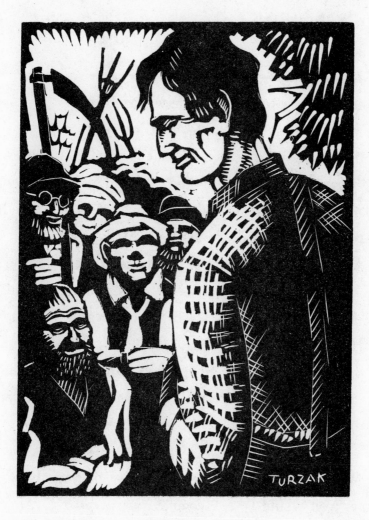

All the time that Abe Lincoln was
   splitting rails,
   and working in a store,
   and bringing people their mail,
   and measuring land,
   and helping to make the laws for Illinois
he was teaching himself to be a lawyer.

In those days, a person did not have to go to school to become a lawyer. He had to read a lot of law books, though, and he had to pass a test. Abe studied hard, and he passed the test.

Abe had borrowed his law books from a lawyer in Springfield, Illinois. Now the lawyer said, "Come to Springfield, Abe. Come and be my partner."

So Abe moved to Springfield and became the partner of John T. Stuart. Abe Lincoln was twenty-eight years old now.

Many years later, a friend asked, "Did you always know you would be a lawyer?"

"No," Lincoln told him. "I didn't know I had enough sense to be a lawyer."

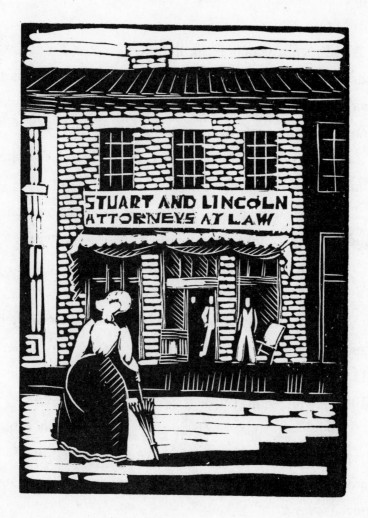

MOVE OVER!

Lawyers in Lincoln's day traveled from one law court to another. Usually they traveled by horse and buggy.

Abe Lincoln was driving his buggy down a narrow road one day when he met another buggy. The road was too narrow for two buggies. One of the two would have to move over.

Lincoln didn't want to move over. If he did, he would get stuck in the mud.

The other driver didn't want to get stuck in the mud, either. "Move over!" he called to Lincoln.

"Move over yourself," Lincoln said.

"I won't," said the other driver.

Very slowly, Lincoln got up in his seat. He looked very tall against the sky. He got taller and taller. "If you don't move over," he said in a loud voice, "I'll tell you what I'll do."

"Please—please don't go any higher," the other driver said. "I'll move over." And he moved over—into the mud. "What would you have done if I hadn't moved over?" he asked.

"I would have moved over myself," Lincoln said, and he drove on.

Abraham Lincoln was an important lawyer now. His old friends still called him Abe, but everybody else called him Mr. Lincoln — or just plain Lincoln.

Whenever he was in court, there was sure to be a crowd. People liked to listen to Lincoln. He could make them understand what he was talking about. And he could make them laugh.

Lincoln was in court one day to help a farmer who had been cheated in a horse trade.

The lawyer for the other side, Mr. Logan, spoke first. He had his shirt on backwards, but nobody noticed it except Lincoln.

Mr. Logan made a long speech about horses. Then Lincoln got up. He turned Mr. Logan around so that everybody could see him.

"Mr. Logan has been talking about horses for an hour," Lincoln said. "But how much do you think he knows about horses if he doesn't even have the sense to put his shirt on right?"

Everybody but Mr. Logan burst out laughing. And Lincoln won the case for the farmer.

Mary Todd was a pretty young lady, with blue eyes and brown hair. She was gay and rich. She loved parties and good times. And she nearly always got what she wanted.

When she was a girl she told her friends, "I want to be the wife of the President of the United States. The man I marry will be President some day."

When Mary Todd was twenty-one, she met Abraham Lincoln. She was sure that he would be President some day. And she made up her mind to marry him.

Lincoln was more than thirty years old now, and people thought it was time for him to get married. Lincoln thought so too. He liked Mary Todd, and he asked her to be his wife.

And so they were married in the year 1842.

Four years later, Lincoln was elected to be a member of the United States Congress in Washington, D.C. Mary was very proud of her husband. She thought he would soon be President.

At last, when he was fifty-one years old, Abraham Lincoln was elected President of the United States. A few months later, in February 1861, he left Springfield for Washington.

Lincoln's friends came to the railroad station to see him off. "Good-bye," they said. "Good-bye, Abe."

The trip to Washington took twelve days. The train made many stops, and Lincoln made speeches to the crowds waiting to see him.

One day the train stopped at the town of Westfield, in New York State.

A little girl named Grace Bedell lived in Westfield. She had written a letter to Lincoln before the election. She said she thought he would look much nicer if he grew a beard. And that is just what Lincoln did.

Lincoln made a short speech in Westfield. Then he asked for Grace Bedell. A man brought her to the front of the crowd. Lincoln stepped down from the train and kissed her. "I let these whiskers grow for you, Grace," he said.

From that time on, Lincoln wore a beard.

President and Mrs. Lincoln moved into the White House with two of their sons. Tad was nearly eight, and Willie was eleven. Another son, Robert, was in college.

People thought the Lincolns spoiled their children. But Mr. and Mrs. Lincoln always said, "Let the children have a good time."

Tad and Willie were noisy and busy from morning till night. They played ball in the White House. They ran into their father's office and jumped on his lap. They dressed up in their mother's clothes and put on shows.

One day Tad made a cart out of a chair, tied two goats to it, and drove through the house. Once he ate all the strawberries that his mother was saving for guests. All his mother said was, "Now what made you do that, Tad?"

A year after the Lincolns moved into the White House, Willie got sick and died. It was a sad time for the Lincoln family.

Right after Lincoln became President, a terrible war began. It was a war between the southern states and the northern states.

The southern states did not want to be part of the United States anymore. They wanted to start their own country, so they could have all the slaves they wanted. The northern states did not want to let the South start a new country. They wanted to keep the United States together.

Abraham Lincoln was on the side of the North. He wanted the country to stay together. And he did not like slavery.

The war made President Lincoln very sad. Sometimes he was so sad that he cried. But President Lincoln still told funny stories to his friends. And sometimes he took a joke book out of his desk and read jokes for a while.

Lincoln's friends didn't understand how he could read jokes or tell funny stories when there was so much to be sad about. Lincoln told them that he needed to laugh. "If I did not laugh I would have to weep," he said.

President Lincoln got some news one day that made him feel happier. Northern soldiers had just won a battle at Gettysburg, Pennsylvania. The North was beginning to win the war.

A few months later, Lincoln came to visit the battlefield at Gettysburg. The place was quiet now. There were rows and rows of graves — the graves of soldiers who had died in the battle.

President Lincoln made a speech. He said people would not remember what he said that day, but they would always remember the brave men who died to keep the United States together.

Lincoln's speech was short — less than three minutes. The people who heard it didn't think it was much of a speech. Lincoln didn't think it was very good, either. He was sorry he hadn't done better.

Years later, people began to think about Lincoln's words again. They began to understand that Lincoln had made a beautiful speech at Gettysburg after all. Now it is one of his most famous speeches.

PRESIDENT LINCOLN IS SHOT

Abraham Lincoln was elected President for the second time in the year 1864. And on April 9, 1865, the war came to an end at last.

The North had won the war. Now the North and the South would stay together as one country. And there would be peace again.

The war had been terrible for both sides. But it was over, and President Lincoln began to look forward to better days. "We have both suffered," he told his wife. "Now let us both try to be happy."

On Friday, April 14, 1865, the President and Mrs. Lincoln went to the theater to see a play. And that night a man with a gun came to the theater and shot the President.

The next morning President Lincoln was dead.

ABRAHAM LINCOLN

Born on February 12, 1809.

Died on April 15, 1865.

President of the United States from March 4, 1861,
to April 15, 1865.